Tires and Testicles

Tires and Testicles

What You Need to Know About

Men and Boys

James Weigand

Illustrated by: Mark Preston

Library of Congress Control Number:		2010906503
ISBN:	Hardcover	978-1-4500-9771-0
	Softcover	978-1-4500-9770-3
	Ebook	978-1-4500-9772-7

This book was printed in the United States of America.

To order additional copies of this book, contact:
Xlibris Corporation
1-888-795-4274
www.Xlibris.com
Orders@Xlibris.com
78462

DEDICATION

Sujen Whong Weigand, your patience, kindness, and support are daily reminders that dreams really do come true.

Acknowledgement

I want to thank everyone who helped to make this book possible. Many people asked questions and encouraged me to write. It is for you that this book has been written. I owe a particular debt of gratitude to the following people: Erin VanTroostenberghe (whose hair salon provided me with so many questions) for insisting I write my answers. Camelot Mayorga, thank you for being a sounding board. You have a wonderful eye and a better ear. Thank you for applying both. Kara Oh, queen of the genre, thank you for your advice and encouragement. Mark Preston, your illustrations kept things light and fun. Jennifer Lewis, I cannot thank you enough for the time and care you have taken in vetting this text.

Contents

"We Need to Talk"

We Need to Talk

If the person you are talking to doesn't appear to be listening, be patient. It may simply be that he has a small piece of fluff in his ear.

—Winnie the Pooh (A. A. Milne)

I have good news for every girl who ever wished she could understand boys. The good news is they are not complicated. I think you will find that boys, most anyway, are a lot less complicated than girls. So have a seat, make yourself comfortable, and give me your attention. I know a thing or two about boys.

I spent a lot of time being a boy. My best friends were boys. I know what they do. I know how they act. I know what they like. I know what they think. And I know what they finally become. So I'm something of an authority on boys. This might get me kicked out of the **Boys Only Club**, but that's a chance I'll just have to take. I'm about to give you the signs, symbols, and passwords to the club. I think everybody will be better off for it.

For more than 20 years, I've listened to teenage girls venting their frustrations about teenage boys. Usually I hear things like, **Why won't he tell me what he's feeling?, Why doesn't he call me?, Why aren't boys more sensitive?, Why don't boys ever see what's beneath the surface?, Why don't boys listen?** You can change the names, and you change the faces of the people who ask those questions, but those questions are always among the perennial favorites.

Let's take a look at the last one. The truth is boys **do** listen. No, not all boys are good listeners all the time. Even your best girlfriend isn't a good listener all the time. And, of course, some people are just better listeners than others. It's a learned skill. It's a skill some people have mastered. And it's a skill some people need to work on. But boys listen just as well as girls. They just listen **differently**.

When your girlfriend listens to you, she interacts with you. Chances are she will nod her head, pat your hand, and punctuate your sentences with little empathic sounds. She hears you. You know she does. She is right there with you, reassuring you that she is taking in everything that you say. Don't expect your boyfriend to do that. When boys have something important to say to a friend, they want full, undivided attention. A boy will very often consider all those little reassuring gestures your girlfriend makes to be **interruptions**. They aggravate him. There is, compared to girls, very little physical activity going on when boys have a serious talk. He looks his friend in the face, and he listens. No **uh-huhs**, no pats on the hand, no **interruptions**; he gives his friend his full, undivided attention. That's what guys do. This is his best buddy. It's important. He can kid him and josh with him later.

The problem is when guys listen to girls, they get an entirely different reaction than when they listen to each other. He looks in your eyes. He sits motionless. He listens. Hey, you are somebody important to him, and you have something real on your mind. He's there. That's when it happens. He gets blindsided. *You're not listening! You don't care* And very often, those accusations are followed by angry tears. Do you think he's confused? You bet he is. That's how guys are wired. That's how they are put together. If you want your boyfriend to listen to you, expect him to listen like a boyfriend. You don't expect a dog to act like a cat. Why would you expect your boyfriend to act like your girlfriend?

Boys are action-oriented. Okay, your fella might be a real couch potato, but his mindset is action. You tell your girlfriend about your tough day or the sales person that was rude to you, and your girlfriend listens. Tell that same story to your boyfriend, and he tells you what to do about it. The problem is you didn't want him to **do** anything about it. You didn't need him to tell you how to deal with it. You just wanted him to listen. Okay, you're feeling upset and it would be nice if he would mirror some of that same feeling, but you didn't want him to **do** anything. Guys don't operate that way. Guys fix it. If you didn't want his advice, why are you telling him all this? That's his reaction. For the most part, boys show affection through action. Boys use less than half the words girls do. He may talk your head off when the two of you are on the phone. If he does, it ought to tell you something because boys are notorious for their abbreviated phone calls. A guy probably wouldn't tell the same story you just told your girlfriend unless he wanted some advice. If you want your guy to just listen, it might be a good idea to tell him up front that's all you want him to do.

So, what does it mean when he won't talk to you? It means he doesn't want to talk about whatever it is he has on his mind. That's a hard notion for a lot of girls to grasp. Girls like to talk it out. Girls may not want advice, but they like to talk about it. Boys are another story. Remember the story you told him about the rude sales clerk? You didn't want his advice on what to do about it. You knew what to do about it. You didn't want advice; he wasn't quite sure why you told him. If he wants advice, he'll ask. You'll know when he wants advice. When boys ask for advice, it comes in the form of a question. It sounds something like this, "does this shirt go with this?", "what movie do you wanna see?", "what time do you think we ought to get there?" In his world, that's asking for advice. Right now, he is mulling over something that's bothering him. **Leave him alone**. Do not, under any circumstances, pressure him to talk about it. That's a good idea for your female friends. It's a bad idea for your male friends. Trust me on this one, ladies. He is not mad at you. That is he's not mad at you, **yet**. Keep asking him what's wrong and he will be mad at you. That sort of pestering almost always results in something unfortunate. Just be there with him. You can hold his hand, but don't pressure him to talk. Just being there with him will mean a lot to him. He wants you to just be there in much the same way you wanted him to just listen. So just be there for him. When he's ready to talk, he'll talk.

A young lady I know had been insisting her boyfriend talk when something was bothering him. That well-intended practice nearly always resulted in a fight. The next time her boyfriend grew silent, she followed my advice and let him have his space. He was quiet as they drove to the mall. They walked through the mall hand-in-hand, yet he scarcely spoke. "On the way home," she reported, "he opened up and nearly talked my head off." So, remember, next time your boyfriend says **he doesn't want to talk about it**, he doesn't want to talk about it. Don't push. I once heard a comedienne come dangerously close to understanding this one while making light of it. She said she had finally figured out what men really want. "They want," she said, "someone who will be really, really close and leave them the hell alone." All kidding aside, when your guy doesn't want to talk, just being there for him makes you really close. You did want to be close, didn't you? When your date pays you a compliment, **please**, don't pooh-pooh it. It's bad form, ladies. Guys put up with it. Most guys are used to it, but they don't like it. It goes something like this, he tells you he likes your new haircut. You say you hate it. Your hair cutter, you say, really messed it up. Bad move, ladies. You just insulted his taste. He **likes** it, remember? You don't have to agree with him. But, please, don't insult his taste. Hey, he likes you enough to ask you out. Is his taste all that bad? I know you want to appear modest. To say, "Yes, I know," would be a real put off. There are, however, alternatives to this response. You could simply say, thank you. Good manners are always in style. You know, of course, that boys can say the most ridiculous things. You're in an old t-shirt and worn jeans. Your face is completely bare of make-up. Your hair is wind blown. This is when he chooses to tell you how pretty you are. I know. He's crazy. He's crazy about you. He doesn't see the best foot forward you. He sees you. And he likes what he sees. Isn't that nice to know? Boys are not very complicated. A lot of boys make very good company, once you know the signs, symbols, and passwords of their world. Now you do.

"A Strange Turn of Events"

A Strange Turn of Events

Two wrongs don't make a right, but three lefts do.

—Jason Love

Rob made up his mind. This was it. This was going to be a special evening. He washed the car and chose his clothes carefully. He made reservations for dinner at a scenic little place in the mountains. It was the perfect spot. The lodge was framed by one of the highest mountain peaks in the state. The leaves were turning, and from where they would sit, they would have a perfect view of the lake. Everything was going to be perfect.

Rob arrived on time to find Carol dressed and waiting. They began the long scenic ride up the mountain. "Now, where exactly are we going?" she asked. Rob was coy. It was a place he had liked as a child. He was sure she would like it too. He hadn't been there in years, but he had talked with a friend who had been there recently just to make sure the food was still good. It was, he was assured.

Nothing could dampen this evening, not even the slow moving lumber truck he found himself behind. He would just have more time to chat to enjoy Carol's company. He was imperturbable.

As the truck pulled its load around the curve and up the hill, the driver shifted gears and stepped on the gas. The truck responded with a cloud of smoke. "Ugh, that's disgusting," Carol said. The cloud dissipated fast enough, but the damage was done. Little dots of black began to appear on the windshield. "What's that?" Rob asked. Without thinking, Rob turned on the sprayer and windshield wiper. Too late, he realized his mistake. The dots spread across the windshield in an oily film. Gone was the perfect evening. Rob leaned forward searching for the road through his oily windshield. Rob felt the muscles in his neck tighten. "There has to be a spot where I can pull over," he said.

Fifteen minutes later, Rob was on the side of the road, sleeves carefully rolled, ruining a handkerchief on his oily windshield. Try as he did, Rob could not avoid getting his shirt dirty. "It will come out," Carol assured him of the oil spots. Rob didn't think so, but that scarcely mattered. The evening was as ruined as his shirt. Now he wasn't sure where his turn was. He couldn't be sure he hadn't passed it.

"Carol," he said, "I think I may have missed the turn."

"Are we lost?" she asked. "Do we need to ask somebody for directions?"

"No," he said, "it's west of here."

"Where is that?" she asked. He gestured to his right. "Okay," she said as though that settled everything.

"Carol," he said patiently, "I still don't know where the turn is . . . I could hardly see the road. If I were a crow, we could fly there."

"It's not a big deal, honey. We can do it another time."

"It is a big deal," he muttered.

"You know the way back . . . don't you?"

"Yes, Carol, I know the way home. I left bread crumbs so we wouldn't get lost." He was getting irritated now. "And it should be real easy in the dark with oil on the windshield." He had thought the sun setting over the lake would be a beautiful site. Now he hated to see the light go.

Carol ignored his snide remarks. "Honey, we can do this anytime. We have forever to do anything we want. When we get home, I'll fix us something to eat."

Carol had a nice way of putting things. There was something permanent and promising in her comment. He liked that. Still, Rob felt somehow defeated. The one night when he really needed to feel like he knew what he was doing, and he wasn't even sure Carol really believed he knew where he was going. "Yeah, honey," he muttered, "you're right. We'll do it another time."

He climbed into the car, and they began the slow descent down the mountain. There was no way Carol could know what he had planned. She could not know he had intended to ask. That would be another day, another setting. Women, Rob thought, could be so perceptive and so clueless all at once. How were they possible, he wondered.

It was a quiet ride back. Carol made a few attempts at conversation. Rob answered in monosyllables and starred through the windshield. Now he would be happy just to get home safely. The evening had turned chilly; Carol would be happy to get back. The only sustained conversation in the car was the one in Rob's head. *How could she have asked if he knew where it was? How could she have asked if he knew the way home?* Maybe she didn't have confidence in him. Maybe it was just as well he didn't get to propose. Maybe he was lucky. **Lucky?!** Some luck he was having. And so the conversation went in his head.

Men can be stubborn about asking directions. They can be a bit touchy, too. So why are men so very different from women in this regard? The answer brings us back to the spatial part of the male brain. This is the part of the brain your guy inherited from the **hunter** among his **hunter-gatherer** ancestors. This is the ancestor that learned to track, trail, and hunt. He developed a keen sense of direction which held him in good stead. The guys that didn't develop this sense of direction got lost. A good sense of direction was a good thing to have.

Women, so the theory goes, had less of a need to exercise this part of the brain than her male counterpart. Instead, nature demanded that women, the gatherer of our hunter-gatherer duo, develop a far greater capacity for speech and language function, and multitasking. Whether or not the hunters and gathers of antiquity are actually responsible for this difference in men and women, I can't say for certain. It is a plausible theory. Whatever the reason, it has been demonstrated numerous times, men, as a group, have a good sense of direction. Men have always placed a large measure of their self-worth on their ability to get results. They place a lot, often an unhealthy amount, of identification and self-worth on their work. What's that got to do with getting lost? Well, if he doesn't know where he's going, he's **lost** and he's not supposed to be lost. With you in tow, he is supposed be caretaker and provider, and he hardly feels that way when he is wandering around in circles. And men hate to admit they're lost. The American pioneer and frontiersman, Daniel Boone, was once asked if he had ever been lost. "No," Boone is supposed to have replied, "but I was once bewildered for three days."

Yeah, it's like that. Heroes don't get lost. They explore. And, yes, they are bewildered from time to time. What can you do about it? Well, for starters, don't encourage him to feel like an imbecile. At the moment, it is a secret fear of his. You'll only make matters worse if you do. If he is into gadgets, GPS systems are nice. I know of one woman who bought her husband one, and set the voice to a sexy Australian woman. He loves using his GPS. One old school ploy is to feign the need for a restroom and ask directions yourself. And maps are still good. Compliment him on his map reading skills, and he just might use it.

It might take a little while, but the good news is most of us still find our way home. Hey, if we didn't, there wouldn't be any ancient ancestors. He'll get there.

Oh, Rob did eventually propose. He and Carol have been married for twenty-one years and have four children.

"Don't You Believe it"

Don't You Believe It

Self-esteem isn't everything; it's just that there's nothing without it.

—Gloria Steinem

Love yourself first and everything else falls into line. You really have to love yourself first to get anything done in this world.

—Lucille Ball

I like our pop culture magazines, print and electronic. They're fun to look at, but I wish that for just one day, we could toss all of them away. Why? Because girls believe what they see in them. They see impossibly perfect physiques and flawless skin. They see models that have been made-up, airbrushed, and computer-enhanced to achieve an awe-inspiring look. It is fun to look at, but it is no more real than a Disney cartoon. Unfortunately, for the people on the receiving end of this media onslaught, it is down right intimidating. The message is that you, dear girl, are supposed to look this way. There is something wrong with you if you don't look this way, and no boy is going to want to date you if you continue to look the way you do. Of course, this intimidation helps to sell products. That's the whole idea.

What is being sold is obvious. There is lipstick for full pouting lips, eye shadow for smoky smoldering bedroom eyes, and foundations for a creamy smooth complexion. Who wouldn't want those things? The women are beautiful. And sometimes, in person, they look **almost** as good as their photographs. But there is more on sale here. **Image** is being sold. You are being told that this person or that person is pretty or sexy (not necessarily the same thing). This is what guys like. This is his type. All guys like this type. Don't you believe it.

There is no one type that all boys like. Grown women have been surprised to find out that popular movie stars and models, often hailed as beautiful and sexy, are not found to be so by some very red blooded men. Who and what they like, let alone why they like them, can be **very** complicated. He probably can't tell you why he likes what he likes. It would in all likelihood take years of thought, therapy, and introspection to figure out why he finds certain types more attractive than others. Most guys are not that introspective. That's fine. You don't need to know why. This is as simple or complicated as driving a car. You don't need to know much about engines to drive a car. You don't need to know why his preferences are what they are. You do need to know that the media does not determine his type. No matter how well the media sells movies and cosmetics, no matter how well the media sells its wares to you—marketing does not determine his type.

That's good news. None of us can be those other people. But let's make no mistake, fame does carry with it a certain kind of appeal. It does get his attention just as it gets yours. There is a notion that somehow, celebrities are a little superior to the rest of us; after all, they are treated differently from the rest of us. They must, therefore, be a little better than the rest of us, or so the reasoning goes. It's not true, of course, but most of us fall prey to this kind of thinking from time to time. These people are, after all, marketed to leave us with just this impression. We are encouraged to think this way. Now, take fame out of the equation, and he is likely to tell you he finds many girls and women he comes across in his everyday encounters just as attractive, if not more so than her more celebrated sisters.

Please keep in mind, his type or types includes more than physical characteristics. Did I say types, **plural**? Yes. A lot of guys have more than one type. No, this does not mean everyone is his type any more than everyone is your type. A lot of guys fail to recognize they have a type. Unless he stops to think of love interests he has had and looks for things they have in common, he is likely to miss the emerging pattern. If you know the romantic history of a male friend, you may be in a better position to see his type than he is. He may even deny he has a type. But he does. And it should be noted his type often evolves as he grows. As he gets older, his type often comes to include attributes, physical and otherwise, he failed to appreciate when he was younger. It may come as a surprise, but he does grow.

So if type is more than appearance, why all the emphasis on looks? It's because guys are visual creatures. It's their nature. Okay, he's also neuro-linguistically programmed for auditory, kinesthetic, gustatory, and olfactory sensations. That is, he's capable of processing information through all five of his senses. That's important. But unless your guy is blind, it's where he starts. It's what gets the game going.

In about five seconds, little more than the time it takes a baseball player to run from home to first, he has formed an impression of you. He finds your face attractive; his eyes drop to your feet and scan up. If you made a good impression, he'll look a second time. If he's interested, he'll look a third time. Whether or not he acts on that interest is another matter.

Why might he not act on his interest? There are a lot of reasons. He might be involved. You might have a ring on your finger. You may not be the only girl to catch his interest. Of course, you may be with your girlfriends. A covey of girls can keep the boys away in droves. He knows that to hook up with you, he has to pass muster with all your friends. He knows it's not likely. He always runs the risk of getting shot down. Taking a risk is one thing. Providing entertainment for all your friends is another. If you want to be approached, you'll have to be approachable. Appearing approachable is all part of the look.

And visual though he is, this isn't all about your good looks. A lot of pretty girls aren't popular with the boys. He sees a lot more than pretty. The way you wear your make-up, move, dress, and gesture, all go through the scanner. It's all part of that first impression. And that first impression is usually pretty accurate.

How can a pretty girl fail to be popular with the boys? In spite of situation comedies to the contrary, **air-heads** rank pretty low on the popular list. I remember a ceremony of dubious awards given out on a college campus. One of the prettiest girls on campus was awarded two big bags of air while the DJ played **Two Thousand and One a Space Odyssey.** The award was for biggest air-head on campus, or a space cadet they were often called. This was a pretty girl that was always hurting for a date.

Also low in the popularity contest is **Miss Loud and Obnoxious.** This girl is pretty. She has a drop-dead gorgeous figure. And the boys talk about her. They talk **bad** about her. They make fun of her. Obnoxious is something they can see. It's not something they like. She's nice to look at, but a little bit of her can go a long way. Thank you, no.

So what makes some girls so much more approachable than others? What do approachable girls know that other girls don't? They know two things . . . It's too simple . . . You're going to kick yourself. They know to make direct eye contact and smile. That's it.

You want to get the party started? Catch his eye. It's unlikely anything will happen until you do. Look straight in his eyes. Hey, this isn't a stare. Staring makes people uncomfortable. This is just direct eye contact. Now, lower your eyes before looking back up. It's important that you look down when you break eye contact. A look to the side says you might find somebody else more interesting. If you want him to come over, that's not the signal to send. Look down, then up. It's a look that says, "Hey, no promises, but I find you interesting."

If you want him to like you—smile. I cannot emphasize enough how important it is to smile. A smile says you're confident. Confidence is sexy. A smile is accepting. Everyone wants to be accepted. A smile says you're happy. We all like being around happy people. It may sound too simple, but a smile can be devastating. Every femme fatale has a killer smile. It's the one thing they all have in common. Why? Because it is the most powerful *ju-ju* she has in her bag of tricks. It works.

The combination of direct eye contact followed by a genuine smile is like a left jab and a hard right. It is bound to get his attention. I saw this attention-getting device masterfully demonstrated several years ago in a little convenience store. The store was in a little college town. The young lady who worked there was ten to twelve years older than most of the coeds. Her waist and diminutive bust must have measured the same. There was nothing physically impressive about here. Yet college boys went to great lengths to get her attention. The girls were baffled by the effect she had on the boys. After all, they were younger, better educated and, in many cases, better looking. What did she know that they didn't? She knew how to make good eye contact. The look was exclusive. It said, "You are the most interesting man in the room. I've got eyes for nobody but you." The boys ate it up. They always do. And then there was the femme fatale's trademark—the killer smile. The boys always smiled back.

That's one of the things about a smile. It's contagious. Try catching someone's eye and flash a smile in passing. Watch them smile back. It happens nearly every time. Of course, there is more to you than just good looks. Do you want him to know it? Smile. A smile sets everything in the best possible light. It's like dinner by candlelight; it just makes everything look better, even those things that aren't physical.

Despite all the visual clues, all the attractions are not physical. There are personality types too. And they figure into the mix in a big way. It's a baffling part of the equation. These attractions can be hard to understand. It's not a matter of opposites attracting. Despite appearances to the contrary, we like people who are like us. We like people who share our interests. We like people who share our values and temperaments. Type is more than a particular look.

Enjoy the magazines, but remember magazines don't determine his taste. There is no one type that all boys find attractive.

"Jumping Through Hoops"

Jumping Through Hoops

Familiarity breeds contempt. Without familiarity nothing gets bred.

—Retort attributed to Sir Winston Churchill

Rachel wasn't getting a lot of sympathy from her girlfriends. She was cute and bubbly, and guys were asking her out. And she was going out—frequently. So what was the problem? In a village filled with Protestants, it was difficult to find a fella who shared her family's religion, and while she was hardly devout, a point her girlfriends reminded her of, it was something she wanted for a long-term relationship. That was the state of things when Rachel met Mordecai.

Mordecai seemed like the answer to Rachel's prayers. He was cute, he was polite, and he shared her family's faith. He lived forty miles away in a major city, but that hardly seemed like an insurmountable obstacle to romance. It was a city Rachel knew and liked. Besides, any time they went out, it was almost bound to be in the city. She would have no problem driving to the city. She did it often enough anyway. Of course, she was thirty and he was ten years her junior, and her friends had already begun to tease her about the age difference. Behind her back, the people, she called friends, made unkind comments about the **cradle robber.** But she would deal with that. The clock was ticking, and she had made up her mind. Sometimes, a girl just had to do what a girl had to do.

So she set her cap for Mordecai. And she did everything right. She met him at the community center where he was playing basketball, something he really enjoyed. She smiled brightly as her brother introduced them. She was the same friendly girl with Mordecai as she was with everyone else. She made that all-important first impression. However, Rachel knew first impressions, no matter how important they were or how well they went, were still just *first* impressions. Something more was needed. She needed to become a familiar face. So Rachel began to show up on Mordecai's personal radar screen. When he went to the food festival, she just happened to be there too. When Mordecai officiated a children's soccer game, Rachel tagged along as the friend of a soccer mom. Friends, of course, reminded her of the old adage about familiarity breeding contempt. But Rachel knew better. After all, unlike some of her girlfriends, she had no trouble getting dates. She knew that to get a guy to ask her out she had to be available. The more she was around Mordecai, the more likely he was to like her, providing of course that the first impression had been good, and it had been. She had even taken care to see that he associated her with happy occasions. Everything went well.

Soon, Rachel and Mordecai were dating. Rachel was ecstatic. She couldn't have been happier. And that is when she began to get it all wrong. In order to get someone to like you, it is necessary to be around that person fairly often. In short, you have to make yourself available. Rachel had gotten all of that right.

So what went wrong? After you go through the **liking stage** and begin dating, things change. Had she wished only to be friends, she could have continued as she was doing indefinitely. The dating dynamic changes everything. Had Rachel treated Mordecai the same way she treated her last suitor, the one she wanted to go away, she would have held Mordecai's attention much more securely. Like so many ladies, she got this part turned around.

Here is what happened. Rachel became *too* available. She baked fresh chocolate chip cookies and took them to Mordecai's games. It seemed she was always baking brownies or fixing dinner for her new boyfriend. If Mordecai called and she had made plans to do things with her girlfriends, instead of explaining she had made plans, she dropped what she was doing and hurried over. She made herself available at his every beck and call. She over did it. By always being available, she devalued herself. She became less appreciated.

Mordecai wasn't being a bad guy. He had had no conscious thought of devaluing Rachel's attentions. That wasn't his idea. He was just being a normal guy. We all tend to take for granted that which is readily available. How many people spend a lot of time thinking about the air they breathe? It's always there. In much the same way, Rachel was always there. And after a while, Mordecai didn't give her a lot of thought either. The point is this—*the value of anything is determined by its scarcity.* Take limestone and diamonds, they are both rocks. Limestone is arguably the more practical of the two. Certainly, the limestone is less expensive and more appropriate for paving a driveway or filling a pothole. And as lavish as a ton of rocks may be, when was the last time that you heard of a man trying to woo a lady with a load of limestone? It seems funny that a small diamond should be seen as a much grander gesture than a whole truckload of limestone, but we know it is. And if you don't want to be taken for granted, you need to start thinking of yourself as a diamond.

This is not to say that none of Rachel's lavish attention was appreciated. Of course it was—*at first*. Mordecai's last girlfriend had not been so demonstrative. Rachel's affection was, by contrast, obvious and refreshing. And had Rachel meted these special attentions out a little at a time, Mordecai would likely have gone on appreciating his girlfriend's devotion. But Rachel taught Mordecai to take her for granted. She made herself as available as the air he breathed. She neglected her friends, hobbies, and interests for Mordecai. She made her boyfriend her whole world. She lost perspective. And that is always a mistake.

Her last boyfriend, Robert, had ceased to hold much interest for her. He was a nice enough guy. She certainly didn't want to hurt his feelings, so she made herself less and less available, hoping to ease him out of her life. She never called him, and she took her time returning his phone calls. If she had made other plans with her girlfriends, she said so. If she had other things she wanted to do, she did them. When it suited her to go out with Robert, she went out. Unwittingly, Rachel was playing hard-to-get with a guy she didn't want. And the more she played hard-to-get, the more attention he paid. Had she treated Mordecai the same way, she would likely have gotten similar results. She, in effect, wooed Robert with a diamond and smothered Mordecai with limestone.

We all want that which we can't have. And we all value most that which we have to work for. Men in particular enjoy the hunt. Mordecai needed, like all men, to be encouraged enough to join the hunt, but he also needed to be challenged enough to stay in the hunt. There is an old joke that makes the point. A boy was getting ready for a date and wondering if he was going to get lucky. His date was also getting ready for their date and **she already knew** if he was going to get lucky. Rachel already knew she would let Mordecai catch her. The problem was she had removed all doubt. Once they had begun dating, Rachel had made things too easy and too predictable.

If you remove all doubt, you will be taken for granted, and your grandest gestures will go unappreciated. So what does he really want? He wants to work at it a little bit. He wants to be reminded of just how desirable you really are. And he wants you to remember it too.

"Let's Go on Holiday"

Let's Go on Holiday

A vacation is what you take when you can no longer take what you've been taking.

—Earl Wilson

Today is Valentine's Day, or as men like to call it, Extortion Day!

—Jay Leno

It was a snowy Thursday morning in Chicago. The date was February 14, 1929. Everyone in Chicago thought Al Capone had something to do with the St. Valentine's Day Massacre. But the mobster had taken care. He had an alibi. While much of rival "Bugs" Moran's North Side Gang was being led to their slaughter, Capone was vacationing thousands of miles away in Miami.

Moran's men were being led to a warehouse on 2122 North Clark Street, where they thought they would be picking up a shipment of smuggled whiskey. Inside, they found three cops and two other men waiting for them. They were busted. They did as they were told and lined up against the wall. That's when the hit men, disguised as Chicago's finest, went to work. They pulled out Thompson submachine guns and fired at the helpless men. Seven of Moran's men died in the massacre. No one ever went to trial for the largest gangland murder in American history.

And what on earth does any of that have to do with your guy? Well, nothing, except that on Valentine's Day, millions of males feel like they have been ambushed. They feel trapped and can't get away. And they are not altogether wrong.

Valentine's Day is a woman's holiday, and every man on the planet knows it. He knows he had better remember it, and he knows he had better do something about it. Flowers seem to be de rigor on this holiday, and your guy has long since discovered the price of flowers is going to be jacked up on the Fourteenth. He doesn't know what they should cost to begin with, but he does know that they will be higher for Valentine's Day. And all that specially wrapped and decorated candy is priced to flatten his wallet too. He knows it. He knows that if he wants to take you to dinner, he better make reservations. And that's no guarantee that there won't still be a long wait. Even those silly balloons seem to cost more than usual.

Of course, all this information has to be factored into an equation that takes into account how long you've been dating and just how involved you are. If he figures wrong and makes the grand gesture too soon, he risks scaring you away. If he does too little, he comes across as cheap or uninterested, and he risks running you away. It's kind of like algebra; he doesn't understand the problem, but he knows he has homework. He's okay with that. He knows this is one of your high, holy holidays. He's been clued in since elementary school, when he gave you that little heart shaped candy that said, "Be My Valentine." He gets it. He knows anniversaries and birthdays are a big deal for you too. And he knows he had better be on hand for New Year's Eve too, if he wants to call himself your boyfriend. All these are women's holidays. He knows that.

Are you aware that men have holidays too? Most girls and women don't get that. They tend to trample his time and dismiss his holidays as unimportant. Of course, he wants to be remembered on his birthday, it would be a mistake to think otherwise, but he doesn't require a big production. He's not 11, and birthdays just haven't been a big deal since. It's little more than another day for most men. If you cook dinner on Valentine's Day and set out some candles, he will probably think you hung the moon, but make no mistake, it's still your day. So what is a man's holiday?

The Super Bowl is at the top of the list for most guys. Even men who don't regularly follow football are likely to observe this one. The day isn't just about football. It's about being with the guys. It's about hotdogs and drinks, buffalo wings and burgers. It's a guy thing, and you're welcome to join in if you like. No? That's fine too. His holidays don't require your participation. Things he buys for his holidays won't be taking a sudden jump in price. If they did, he wouldn't buy them. There is nothing you have to buy, nothing you have to do. All you have to do is understand it's his turn.

One young lady I know didn't understand that. Her fellow, a former college football player and coach, was trying to watch the Super Bowl when she decided the Christmas decorations had to come down. Why they were still up in February, I didn't ask, but they had to come down right then. Of course, he said he was willing to help just as soon as the game was over. That wasn't soon enough. She put everything away and then got in a huff over doing it all herself. They laugh about it now, but the whole thing could have been avoided if she had understood it was his day and his turn.

There are other holidays too. Some guys get caught up in March Madness. If your fellow follows basketball, this is his time. And October brings about another time honored holiday—the World Series. If your man observes this time, he will happily give himself over to sleep deprivation for about a week. For some guys, the world all but stops for opening day of hunting season. If he's a hunter, he will wake up before God, perch in a tree, and risk frostbite just for a shot at Bambi. It's his day. But have no fear; in none of these holidays do you need to participate. Perhaps that is why so many women fail to recognize male holidays for what they are. Male holidays don't look like female holidays. It probably doesn't help that they are not the same for all men. Different men have different interests. But whatever his interests, his day will not require you to rob your piggy bank. Your holidays require the presence of a member of the opposite sex. His don't. He probably won't ask you to wade in a trout stream for him. Unlike your holiday, **not** requiring your presence on this occasion is not a slight.

You have Valentine's Day, birthday, and anniversary. (Incidentally if you have made it through middle school you should know by now that anniversary means it happens **annually**. There is no such thing as a two-month anniversary. So, no fair asking him to perform a trick every time you have a sentimental moment.) He knows what is required of him on your days. So what is required of you on his days? Just this—play nice. That's all. He'll love you for it.

One Thing at a Time

Experts say you can't concentrate on more than one task at a time.

—Marilyn vos Savant

I believe that one can indeed work on two or more tasks at once, but in ways yet to be understood.–

—Marilyn vos Savant

I saw it coming. It was a meltdown worthy of a B-grade comedy. He was a buttoned down, everything in its place, anal-retentive type guy. He was being approached about a number of things all at once. Everyone seemed to be asking a question or making a request at the same time. It was a chaotic scene. Try as he did, he just couldn't make order out of such chaos. Finally, he blurted out, to no one in particular, "I can't do fifteen things at once. I'm not a woman!" It was a startling statement. The crowd quieted, and he began to fashion an order out of the requests.

It was a strange statement, but I knew just what he meant. Men and boys are not by nature multitaskers. Most just can't seem to do more than one thing at a time and do it very well. There are efficiency experts and others of that ilk that insist that no one can multitask. All those experts, at least the ones that I know about, just happen to be men. That may be worth noting. I point it out because most of the women I know insist they can, and often do, perform multiple tasks at once. Maybe it's nature's way of preparing young women for the myriad responsibilities of motherhood. I really can't say. I can say women can multitask and men can't.

Let me tell you a story that may illustrate the point. My friend Wally came home from work one day. Excited by some news he had heard in town and certain his wife, Mary Jane, could hear him from the front of the house, he began talking. As he entered the kitchen, he discovered his wife on the phone, cooking dinner, and nursing the baby. She turned, answered him, and returned to the business at hand. Astounded, Wally raised his hands over his head and laughingly kowtowed as though before an eastern potentate. Wally had just witnessed multitasking at its finest. He laughed because he could not imagine attempting what he had just witnessed. Oh, he could have gotten everything done, but he would never have gone about the way Mary Jane did. Most men have not had Wally's experience. Most men find the idea of multitasking just a little suspect. Oh, they can flit from task to task, and those with attention deficit disorder often do, but that is hardly multitasking. And since they can't multitask, somewhere in the back of their minds, they wonder if you really can.

You know that you can multitask, you do it all the time, but do you really know that he can't? Some women find it hard to believe that men can't multitask. Indeed, they find it irritating. It can feel as though he is deliberately trying to do less than his share or doing it slowly when you are trying to hurry. Here is a little experiment for you. Go up to your father, brother, boyfriend, some significant male in your life, whom you might have occasion to see brushing his teeth. Ask him to do something that only requires one hand, while he is brushing his teeth. Don't prompt him. Give no hints that this is an experiment. My guess is that he will stop brushing his teeth, if only for a moment, to do what you ask.

So what does this have to do with you? If you want a boy's attention, don't ask for it while he is attempting to do something else. You'll be disappointed with the results. He's not up to it. Remember the last time you tried to talk to him while he was watching TV? My guess is it wasn't the most scintillating conversation the two of you have had. I know, you can watch TV, talk on the phone, and do your nails all at the same time. So why can't he pay attention to you while he does two other things? Because he's not your girlfriend, he's your guy.

You're confident you can do several things at once. He can't. You know that now. You know how frustrated you felt when he attempted to watch TV and talk to you at the same time. You may be able to talk on the phone, watch television, fold the laundry, and talk to him all at the same time. But he just might not believe it. He just might think he's getting short shrift in the attention department. You don't want that to happen, either. Guys are just as needy for attention as girls are. If he has your attention, let him know. Attention can be very flattering, and that's a good thing.

Put It Down and Step Away Men and Boys in the Bathroom

Men who consistently leave the toilet seat up secretly want women to get up in the middle of the night and fall in.

—Rita Rudner

It was a picnic. Mom, Dad, and the kids were enjoying their chicken and deviled eggs beside a white-capped brook, when little Junior announced he had to use the bathroom. There was, of course, no restroom in sight. They were, after all, outdoors. It was a beautiful day, and Mom had planned for everyone to be outside enjoying it together. But when nature calls, nature calls and cannot safely be ignored. Fortunately for all concerned, Mom knew of a port-a-john tucked away from view by a grove of trees.

She sent Junior off in the direction of the trees. Moments later, she decided she had best oversee the whole adventure from a discreet distance. What she discovered surprised and amused her. Junior was not even in the port-a-john but stood outside peeing on a tree. Why on earth he was doing this she could not imagine. As it turned out, the port-a-john smelled badly, and the boy had no need to sit down. He saw no need to suffer in an unpleasant little box. Junior stepped outside, found a tree, and took aim. He was simply doing what the male of the species had been doing for millennia.

Until quite recently, about a 100 years ago, more or less, depending on the neighborhood, the family restroom was one of the outhouses. Women went together for security reasons, and men fended for themselves. A man who needed to urinate never bothered to use the Johnny house, but peed on a tree or bush or whatever seemed reasonably private and convenient. It was one of the advantages of being a man. It was the norm. Indeed in seventeenth century London, the city supplied pissing posts for the convenience of passers by. And it was convenient for **men**. The point is not to suggest that London was a particularly foul or filthy city. It was; so were many others. The point is that not until the late nineteenth century was an indoor toilet even available.

Men and boys have since that time, out of deference to Mom and Sis, and with Mom's frantic urging, learned to pick up the seat. And thank Mom, he has learned. Without her, many a man would foul his own nest. He has learned to pick up the seat. Most have not learned to put it back down. And that is a source of irritation for many women.

If he does not now put down the seat, don't expect him to start. He picked the seat up, and in his mind, it seems little enough for you to put it down. You don't pick it up for him when you finish. You've fallen in? He never has. He put the seat down. Yes, of course, he put it down for himself. And he thinks you can do the same. He remembered. Can't you? And now, you are ready to fight. Don't. Whether or not he is correct in his thinking is **not** the point here. The point is, it's how he thinks. He is not being passive aggressive or obstinate in his behavior—not over this. It really does seem trivial and unimportant to him. To him, if this is all you have to be upset about, you have little to be upset about, or you enjoy too much finding things to complain about. He may or may not be correct in his thinking, but it is what he is thinking. And you are not likely to change his thoughts. So what are you to do, aside from putting the seat down? I have an idea.

I would like to offer a humble compromise I learned from a doctor. The doctor went into this bathroom to brush his teeth. He couldn't find his brush. His wife had put the all the toothbrushes in the medicine cabinet. Why on earth had she done that, he wondered?

As it turns out, the good doctor's wife was responding to an article she had read. It seems bacteria from the toilet bowl sprays some fifteen feet when flushed. Bacteria from fecal matter and urine could be splattered all over the family toothbrushes. The lady had a point and a good solution. The doctor took advantage of the situation to solve an area of long-standing contention between them. Why not, he suggested, simply put the lid down on the toilet seat after each use. Then the brushes could safely remain out. He now puts the seat down and covers it. Problem solved. They have, as the saying goes, lived happily ever after. So can you.

"Signals"

The Signals You Send

As you think, so shall you be.

—Proverbs

I speak two languages, Body and English.

—Mae West

Brian was in the habit of taking his shirts to the cleaners every Wednesday. There was nothing unusual about this particular Wednesday. Brian parked his car and sauntered into the cleaners. He plopped a week's worth of shirts on the counter.

Bonita was a new employee at the cleaners. She stepped up to the counter and began collecting Brian's shirts. She sorted and counted them. "Name? Phone number? Starch?" She asked. As she looked up from her pad, Brian found himself looking straight into her eyes. Bonita had big, beautiful, brown eyes. Without so much as a thought, Brian smiled. It was a friendly face Brian found himself smiling at. Bonita tucked a bit of hair behind her ear, and smiled back before dropping her gaze to the counter.

Bonita began tapping numbers on the calculator. Brian reached for his wallet. He remembers making some inane comment about the oppressive heat in the place. The cleaners always seemed unbearably hot in the summer. Bonita remembers nodding her head and making some comment about the large fan in the corner. There was nothing important about what either said. Yet somehow, that they had spoken at all seemed important.

As Bonita counted back the change, her hand brushed Brian's. Again, she looked up, almost shyly. And again, Brian found himself smiling as he looked into those big brown eyes.

What had transpired in the cleaners had taken less time than it had taken Brian to walk across the parking lot. Brian chided himself for thinking anything had happened at all. A pretty girl had smiled at him. Nothing more, he told himself. He didn't even know that girl's name, let alone anything about her. She was a pretty girl with a friendly face. She probably smiled like that at everyone. And yet something had happened back there.

Unwittingly, Brian and Bonita had just completed the five steps body language experts Allan and Barbara Pease describe as critical to starting any new relationship. Let's take a look at what just happened.

First, there was eye contact. A great deal took place right there. So what did the eyes tell us? When Brian saw Bonita, he liked what he saw. His pupils dilated. Those dilated pupils were a dead give away that Brian found Bonita attractive. He had no control over that. It happened without conscious thought. This is called an autonomic reflex. It is the same reflex that caused you to blink when trash flew into your face. It caused your pupils to narrow when the sun was too bright. And it is the same reflex that caused your pupils to dilate when the room was too dark. Brian had no more control over his pupils dilating than you did. He might have decided to play it cool and feign disinterest, but had Bonita known what to look for, his eyes would have given him away.

The second of the five steps was the smile. Brian made a terrific first impression. And all he did was smile. That smile accomplished a number of things for him. It said he was happy and confident. That was attractive. It offered acceptance. Everyone wants to be accepted. And it showed enthusiasm. Brian's enthusiasm was contagious. Bonita returned his smile without a moment's thought. Brian and Bonita were off and running.

Bonita preened. That was step number three. She tucked a bit of hair behind her ear. It was one of those little gestures we've all made when we wanted to look good for the opposite sex. When we smoothed our hair, straightened our tie, tugged at a cuff or picked at a piece of lint, we were preening. Bonita never thought about what she was doing or what it meant.

Brian made some comment about the heat. He might have said *hi*, *hello*, or *what's your name*. It all would have accomplished the same thing. Nothing fancy was needed, no poetry, no philosophy. The important thing was that they spoke. It took care of the fourth requirement.

The fifth step was so subtle, it could have been an accident. It wasn't. As Bonita counted back Brian's change, she allowed her hand to brush his. Their hands touching raised the level of intimacy. Had Brian taken the opportunity to introduce himself, Bonita might have shaken hands with him. Bonita needed an opportunity to touch Brian. She found it.

Body language is a fascinating thing. It can be quite revealing and helpful under a number of circumstances. But one needs to be careful. The temptation is to get caught up in reading signals and when one should be thinking more about the signals they are sending. Bonita was fortunate. She was too caught up in the moment to think about Brian's body language. She was taking an order and making change. What was more important for Bonita, though she wasn't aware of it, were the signals she was sending Brian.

Bonita caught Brian's attention with her eyes. Brian responded. When Brian smiled, Bonita smiled. Her body language unconsciously reflected his. And his body language said, he liked what he saw. It was that mirroring, that happy reflection of Brian's own body language, that left him with the feeling that something had just happened at the cleaners, though he wasn't quite sure it wasn't his imagination. It was enough for Brian to seek out Bonita on his next trip to the cleaners.

A woman's success in attracting a man is directly related to her ability to signal her interest. It also depends, of course, on her potential mate's ability to pick up on those signals. And as often as not, men are slow about catching their cues. That may have something do with why women send so many more signals than men. Most women hit men with a barrage of signals within the first few minutes of meeting. The problem comes when those signals are at odds with one another. That's when men become confused and discouraged.

The women who have the most success attracting men are the ones most accomplished at signaling their interest. It is, except among the most brazen, a subtle process. It is a process that leaves men feeling like they are the pursuers. And pursue they do. Pursuing is something men enjoy. But rarely do men initiate the courting rituals. Men don't like to admit it, even to themselves, but most encounters between men and women are initiated by women.

The trick, if it can be called that, is to send good signals. Good signals are clear messages, but they do much more than that, they make you look better. They really do. Let's look at an example. We are looking at a party. Stephanie is perched on the arm of a chair. She is cute and wholesome. Stephanie is the girl next door. Randy has just said something funny. Stephanie throws her head back. Her throat is exposed and her mouth is open in an obvious laugh. Her arms are straight, her hands flat against the arm of the chair, raising her shoulders and pushing her breasts together. Her legs are spread, and her toes are pointed skyward. Suddenly, the girl next door is **hot**. It is spontaneous and innocent. She is still the cute wholesome girl next door. But, **wow**, look at her now! The girl is devastating. Men think about how good looking she is. The same girl walked through the mall earlier that same day, wearing the same jeans and the same t-shirt, and no one gave her a second look. What happened?

Stephanie sent a cluster of signals, and they all said the same thing. They said she was available and interested. Her interest and availability made her more attractive to Randy. In a matter of seconds, Stephanie went from the girl no one was paying attention to, to the girl who ran the room and held Randy's attention for the rest of the night.

What signals did Stephanie send and what did they say? Stephanie's body language said trust, openness, and acceptance. It would have been difficult not to have found her appealing. The head, tossed back, exposed her throat. The throat is a vulnerable area. It is also a highly erogenous area. The mouth was open in an obvious laugh. If Stephanie's smile says she is a happy confident girl, an enthusiastic girl who is willing to accept the individual she is smiling at, and it does, a genuine laugh is a smile squared. Of course, this is not to suggest that Stephanie goes around giggling and laughing at every lame joke or comment that comes her way. Girls who do that are thought of as silly and not very good company. Stephanie's laugh is genuine. It is appealing. Boys have long known that girls who like them are an easier audience for a joke than girls who don't. It is one of the things that girls do to create a bond with the guys they fancy.

For how long have we known the appeal of lips? Pouting and parted lips serve as what animal and human researcher Desmond Morris describes as "self mimicry" of the female genitalia. The ancient Egyptians were keenly aware of the powerful and subtle suggestions the lips could make millennia before Jesus walked the earth. They are the people that invented lipstick. It imitates the swelling of the readied vaginal lips. Stephanie's lips are parted as she laughs. It is the genuine version of the posed look in so many magazines.

Stephanie has pressed her hands against the arm of the chair, pushing her breasts together. Unlike the lingerie models who are skillfully clad and posed to create the look of bountiful breasts and cleavage, Stephanie is wearing a t-shirt. She is fully covered, and yet the effect is the same. In a matter of seconds, Stephanie has transformed herself, and only for a matter of seconds, but it is enough to leave Randy with a favorable impression of her charms. Stephanie is far from being a lingerie model, and yet, she has made as much of her assets as the models.

Stephanie is straddling the arm of a chair. Her legs are parted down either side of the arm. She has gleefully kicked up her heels as she has tossed back her head in a laugh. The posture is inviting.

It is important to note here that Stephanie's signals were being read collectively. It would be a mistake to choose one signal from the many being displayed and try to make sense of it. This time, Stephanie's signals were all in agreement. But that is not always the case. That's why experts recommend looking at several clues before arriving at a conclusion. To hone in on just one signal to the exclusion of all others and without regard to the context under which it is being given can lead to some erroneous notions. It is a bit like pulling one word from a sentence and expecting to grasp the meaning of the entire sentence. That is why body language experts recommend reading signals in clusters. Many recommend looking for as many as four signals before coming to a conclusion. And let's remember, Randy was reading Stephanie's body language the way most people would—**intuitively**. He was **not** consciously aware of what he was reading. Still, Randy was getting the message. For Randy, Stephanie was approachable, and he knew it.

Stephanie's interest in Randy made her more attractive to him. For Stephanie, reading body language was not nearly as important as writing it. Stephanie might have memorized some body language signals to make herself more appealing or to at least ensure she was not sending unwanted signals. That is possible, and there is value in it. But for Stephanie, the *trick* started in her head. Stephanie liked Randy. She was open to his advances, and it showed. What was in her head was reflected in her body's posture. So if Stephanie's thoughts created her body language and her body language made her more attractive, why doesn't everyone's body language make them more attractive? The answer is simple. The body is indeed the outer reflection of what is going on inside. But everyone does not have Stephanie's clarity and confidence. There is no argument going on in Stephanie's head. There is no conversation in her brain that sounds like, "I think I like him, but I'm not sure." There is no thought that, "he is so cute, he would never be interested in me." Such thoughts lead to mixed and confusing signals, signals that can keep the boys away. A great beauty can become her own worst enemy by sending mixed signals or signals that flatly say stay away. Stephanie knows better. She has something else going on inside. Stephanie has confidence. She knows that her most powerful sex organ is her brain. All sex appeal, or the lack of it, starts in the head. Stephanie has a good self-image. She thinks Randy might very well find her attractive. She's a nice girl. She's cute. She's personable. Girls with a lot less to offer have done well with the boys. Stephanie intends to do just as well.

So does Randy get a say in any of this? Of course, he does. Men, after all, are not items on a shelf to be tossed in a shopping cart. Stephanie has initiated the same courting ritual we saw with Brian and Bonita. Stephanie has gotten the ball rolling. Now, it's Randy's turn. The ball is in his court. Randy has his tastes, his interests. If he is interested, he'll pursue Stephanie. He might ask for her phone number. He might ask her out. And there is a very good chance he will leave the party thinking he initiated everything. Guys are like that.

So how do you send the signals that attract the boys and transform your appearance? You can learn a series of poses and postures to get their attention. Such tricks actually work when practiced enough to appear natural. Actresses do it all the time. But it is acting, it is contrived and like some crash diet, it is a temporary fix. Of course, if you find you're hugging yourself, arms crossed in defense or defiance, you might want to ask yourself why and change your posture. There is a world of difference between a clenched fist and an open hand. Both reflect a state of mind. One is appealing; one is not. Do what Stephanie does. Develop a healthy ego. A healthy ego is reflected in your body language. Who you attract into your life is determined in large measure by how you think of yourself. Which, of course, determines the signals you send. So, think well of yourself, and remind yourself of all the reasons you have to think well of yourself. As our modern day philosopher, Dr. John Martini reminds us, "If you don't plant flowers in your garden, you will be forever pulling weeds."

"As Is Sale"

The As-Is Sale

*Never underestimate your power to change yourself. Never
overestimate your power to change others.*

—H. Jackson Brown, Jr.

I was browsing in a furniture store the other day. I like furniture; I
had time to kill, and this seemed like a good place to kill it. So I decided
to take a look. As I walked along, I came across a nice end table. It was
a dark cherry, almost mahogany in color, well-made and reasonably
priced. Of course, the look of the thing caught my attention first. If it
hadn't had been so well made in the first place, I never would have
looked the second time. But it was, and I looked closer. That's when I
noticed the price. It had a good **price**.

End tables seldom go for what I think they ought to. I was once, for
a short time, among the many roles I have played, a furniture salesman.
I learned that end tables usually have a pretty high mark up. Beds can
be found at a reasonable price, and even the matching dresser might be
found to be reasonable. End tables, though, are often a different story. Beds
and dressers are supposed to cost more than end tables; they're bigger
and more essential to one's bedroom. You expect to pay more. You pay
good money for the big-ticket item, and the smaller piece doesn't look
so expensive. It's not likely you'll know the mark up. And so they make
their money. You get a good price on one item; they make it up on the
other item. It's kind of like the overpriced drink that went with dinner.
So what was the story on this end table? It had a **scratch** on it.

There was a big hand printed sign taped to the side, **As Is**. Those two
words said it all. Take this one home, buddy, and you keep it. See the

scratch? We warned you. No getting home and bringing it back because you can't deal with the scratch. Hey, it's a good price, but you have to be able to live with the scratch. Can you live with the scratch?

Now that's something I wish girls understood about boys. They come **As Is.** Boys and men are no different from girls and women in that regard. They want to be accepted for who they are, for what they are. They don't want to be changed. If he wants to change, he'll change. He is quite capable of breaking bad habits or learning good ones. He is also quite capable of telling you he has changed for you. A lot of guys have gotten a lot of mileage out of that story, but for the most part, it isn't true. You stretch the truth to make him feel good about himself, and he stretches it to make himself look good to you. It is a silly little dance we do.

Yes, you might get him to put the seat down on the commode. He might even learn to take out the trash without you reminding him. When I say you are not going to change him, I mean in any meaningful way. *You are not going to change who he is.* Who he is at heart remains the same. If you like him, accept him for who he is. Every one wants to be accepted. It's just a fact of life. If you can't accept him for who he is, you can't begin to love him. Boys don't like being seen as *potential*. And they really resent the notion that they need fixing. He has his faults, and you have yours. So who decided you should find and fix his faults? At best, he finds this attitude presumptuous. At worst, he feels hurt. Just remember that this isn't about his potential. This isn't about molding him into who you would like him to become. This is about who he is. It's **As Is**, lady. They all come with scratches. Can't deal with the scratches? Don't take him home.

"The Chase Scene"

The Chase Scene

Don't call us; we'll call you.

—an American cliché

I realize we live in a modern world, in as much as each generation thinks itself modern. I also realize that, in the Western Hemisphere anyway, today's woman is a liberated woman, at least comparatively speaking. It is, by-and-large, acceptable for today's woman to be strong, assertive, and self-assured. There is no good reason for her not to be. In fact, I don't know of any reasonable man anywhere that would want it any other way. We live in a world with opportunities far different and far more rewarding than those of previous generations. But somehow these opportunities have led to some inappropriate liberties or unfortunate mistakes that may adversely affect the development of a relationship.

The new liberties of modern life have come to mean, for many women, the pursuit of the male. It hasn't worked out so well. It really should be no surprise when you consider that young girls who chase boys are usually not the strong, self-assured ladies of their generation. It is quite the contrary. Historically, girls who chase boys are considered by both sides of the gender-divide to be desperate. We view them as having sold themselves short by not valuing themselves enough to be pursued. By putting themselves in this category, they are much more likely to find themselves taken advantage of. They grow up to become the women, often quite pretty, who are always complaining that boys never treat them right. And they don't. Even the nice guy feels an almost inherent pull to do them wrong. Confident girls, by contrast, are seen as sexy. They are held in high esteem. They are not always the best looking girls, but then they don't have to be. They are strong, self-assured women. They don't have to ask men out. These women expect men to ask them out, and given proper encouragement and opportunity, men generally do. These women treat themselves with respect. They expect the men in their lives to treat them with respect, and they follow suit. So what do these women know?

They know that men haven't changed from time eternal. Laws, times, and technological advancements change, but men remain the same from generation to generation. And that's good news. It means you can discover what makes the men in your life, or the man you want in your life *tick*. Like the laws of nature, men are understandable. I don't want to suggest that men are as predictable as the sunrise, but they can be understood with minimal effort on your part.

What makes men understandable is a sort of male wiring, or as one young man recently expressed it, "a common basic blueprint." Let me let you in on a little secret. Guys don't like to be pursued. They like to do the pursuing. It is how they're wired. Perhaps it harkens back to the days of hunting and gathering. Who is to say? I can say, however, that men still like to think of themselves as the ones doing the pursuing.

Does this mean you are not to be strong and self-assertive? No. By all means, be as strong and as assertive as you desire. Be aggressive, if that's your thing, but understand that the smart, self-assured woman still allows the man to do the chasing.

Yes, we are flattered when you call. Yes, we are flattered when you ask us out. It's always flattering to be considered desirable. But the truth remains—we like to do the calling. We like to do the asking out. We like to think all that stuff is accomplished by us. On some level, we realize that it is not our skill or about our sexual prowess that wins you over, but we like to think so. It's all part of the courtship in our minds. And ladies, it is an important part. What romance is for you, the chase is for the man in your life. Please understand this. Get out your highlighter and highlight this point.

You wouldn't want to be deprived of your romance. Then don't deprive him of his pleasure in chasing you. Don't shortchange him. If you chase him, he will run. That's not good. That is essentially putting the cart before the horse. You don't have to be mechanically inclined to see how well that doesn't work. ***You want him to chase you***. It is important that he chases you. It is important for numerous reasons, one of which is that it establishes a level of value to you and to the relationship. Surely, you are familiar with the notion that anything worth having doesn't come easy? There is a widely accepted correlation between hard work and high value. When you remove the chase from the relationship, you remove the struggle, and thereby minimize your worth in the eyes of your love interest.

Even with this, there are a lot of young women who still don't get it and continue to chase guys. I tell them not to do it, and they don't listen. Their girlfriends tell them not to do it, and yet they persist. Maybe the problem is in the language. Maybe all this talk about **catching** a good guy communicates to them that they need to chase one. I guess it sounds a bit like running down a fly ball. I assure you that this is an entirely different kind of catch. I tend to believe that they are just impatient. I can't say for sure, but the thinking seems to go something like this— "I'm a big girl now. I haven't been living under a rock. I know what turns on a guy's lights." So she chases him with incessant phone calls, unannounced visits, and dates that she initiates. What a great idea this is! I'll bet she also believes that she can make a million dollars by investing seven hours a week in the newest multi-level marketing scheme. Please listen. As tempting as it may be, don't ever chase a man. If you do, I can promise you that one of two things will happen. He will run, and you will feel foolish and rejected, or he will let you catch him, and you will really feel foolish and more rejected. Why? Because in short order, he will run after someone who will encourage him to chase.

Now all of this is not to say that you are totally at his mercy—just a passive participant in the courtship. There is a wide array of things you can do to hype your value and, thereby, increase his interest and move the chase along.

Remember when you were a little girl and you punched or teased some boy to get him to chase you? Things haven't changed much. You still have to tease to get him to chase you. So concentrate your efforts on providing him with all the encouragement he needs. It's how he knows it is okay to pursue you. So play "drop the hanky," "wink," and, by all means, flirt. Flirt your butt off, if you like. Come on strong or be subtle. You decide. Just get the ball rolling. He wants to know he can chase you. He wants to know he can catch you. It is a bit like playing tag, and he is it. It's an easy game to play. You would be surprised at how far a simple smile will take you.

Ohhh, you don't play those games? Well, you and your girlfriends enjoy sharing that bucket of popcorn at the movies. You see, if he doesn't think you want to go out with him, he definitely won't ask you out. It's pretty simple really. Any male old enough to have lived through puberty knows a thing or two about rejection. He avoids it at all cost, and so will be looking for some sort of sign.

You say he's not picking up the signs? Since men aren't that smart, missing a sign or two is possible. You're now thinking that maybe you'd better call him? Wait. Don't touch the phone. Think about this first. He may not be missing the hint at all. What if he didn't miss your signals but genuinely isn't interested, and now you're all out there ringing his phone? That's not going to feel good. You do not have "desperate" written on your forehead, but that move will put it there in red ink. Step away from the phone. Of course, he may have gotten the hint, and he may like the idea. Do you really want to call him first? Do you want to deprive him of initiating the chase? Do you want to miss out on the joy of having him make the first move?

Okay, he asked for your number. He said he would call. That was two days ago. What was that all about? I know guys can take their sweet time about calling. There are a bunch of reasons why they take so long. Entire books have been written about the subject. I won't go into it in depth here, but maybe it will help if I let you in on a little secret. Sometimes, you run across a guy that adheres to what we in the boys club call the forty-eight hours rule. If he is one of those guys, he is not going to call you right away. There is a joke from a show called **Defending the Caveman** that explains things nicely. The joke goes something like this—when a woman says she will call, she means when she gets home. When a man says he will call, he means before he dies. It is hyperbole, of course, but it does have a touch of truth to it. There are reasons for waiting. He knows that if he calls right away, he may appear too anxious. He knows that appearing needy or anxious is a just as unattractive to you as it is to him. He'll wait a day or two to call. He'll play it cool. He'll think about it for a while until he gets his conversation right. If it has been a couple of days and he still thinks it's a good idea, then he'll call.

I'm sorry ladies, but sometimes for reasons you will never be able to fathom, in the face of all attraction, he will choose not to call. Maybe he's lost his nerve. Maybe he decided to ask out somebody else. It doesn't matter what the reason is. You are not to call him. So what do you do? Well, you could just wait until you run into him again. That will usually spur re-interest and make him question why he didn't call you the first time. Many women are familiar with those unintelligible conversations where the man says, "Now, why didn't we ever hook up?" And you look at him like . . . "because you didn't call, stupid." The other option is that you set your cap for somebody else and forget about the guy who was either stricken with amnesia or too shy to call. Either way, you win.

"The Remote"

The Remote

"Men are simple things. They can survive a whole weekend with only three things: beer, boxer shorts, and batteries for the remote control."

—Diana Jordan

What is it about men and the remote control? It is one of the perennial questions women have about men. It's not so much that he must be in charge of the remote that is so bothersome as his insistent clicking from channel to channel that women find so irritating. You don't hear of women driving their spouses wild with constant channel surfing. Clearly, this is male behavior and fairly recent behavior at that. It's not like men have been channel surfing for millennia. Why less than fifty years ago the closest thing dear old dad had to remote control was to have junior hop up from the couch and turn the knob to one of three channels. And yet the explanation probably does lie somewhere back in antiquity.

So what exactly is going on with men and the remote? To answer that question, we need to look at how men think and have thought for eons. The male brain is solution oriented. When the male perceives something to be a problem, his brain quickly seeks to find a solution to the problem and move on. It is a one thing at a time process. No matter how many problems he has before him or how rapidly he discharges them, the mental process is the same—one thing at a time. To think of several things at a time is distracting and irritating. Women on the other hand are multitaskers. Rather than juggling tasks as the harried male might do, her mind is actually dealing with several things at once.

There are some plausible speculations as to why male and female brains work differently. One theory has it that the female with her childbearing and nurturing role needed the ability to multitask in order to keep up with her offspring. It is the same line of reasoning that explains the female's peripheral vision. Women have more peripheral vision than men. She can see farther from side to side without moving her head than her male counterpart which, as the reasoning goes, helps her keep up with her children. That, of course, explains why she can inconspicuously check out every man in the room and her date is likely to be discovered if he is looking at another woman.

His narrower focus, one-thing-at-a-time thinking, and his narrower field of vision may account for his superior depth perception and a more acute sense of spatial relationships. These things were thought to have aided him in his role as hunter-gatherer, provider, and protector of his family. It may also explain why he finds parallel parking less bothersome than most women. Whether or not those theories are right, the fact remains—men and women access and process information differently. Simply put, the male and female brains are not the same.

Which brings us back to the issue of the remote control. Your guy, with his hunter-gatherer brain of yore, flicks through the channels quickly sizing them up. The same brain that once determined in an instant the distance of his prey, the direction of the wind, and the difficulty of the shot now passes judgment on the networks' programming. And he does it as rapidly as any hunter or warrior. What's this program about? What's the solution? Is it predictable? Click. Next. It can be maddening. He doesn't mean for it to be, nor does he mean to hog the remote. He may very well offer it to you only to begin telling you which channels to go to. It's crazy.

Now, he is doing it again. He's doing it again! He's clicking through all the channels he just scanned five minutes ago. What's up with that? Is this some sort of passive aggressive behavior designed to make you crazy? No, it's not. Imagine your man of some millennia ago. He is sitting around the fire with his boys sipping the suds of old. He enjoys the passive entertainment of fire gazing. It is a mindless activity, much like watching television. It allows him to relax and decompress . . . much like television. He stares into the fire. He listens to the crackling of the fire. What's that he hears? Is that the fire or did something move? Is that some nocturnal animal he hears? He scans the horizon before returning his gaze to the fire . . . and so he stares at the TV and surfs the channels, just in case something has changed, in case there is something out there worth his while, in case there is something new on the horizon.

Are there any solutions? There may be a few. You could watch different televisions. That is neither fun nor romantic, but possible. The two of you could decide to play nice and take turns. Of course, you could decide to get off the couch and go do something. You're big people; you figure it out.

"Why Men are Reluctant to Commit"

Why Men Are Reluctant to Commit

Usually, the women gain security and the men have to provide the security. Also after the marriage, the intimate relationship changes, and the husband is no longer getting wild unmarried sex, just boring missionary sex that he has to beg for to get once a month. Women change after marriage, men don't.

—Dayna Thomas

Women marry men hoping they will change. Men marry women hoping they will not. So each is inevitably disappointed.

—Albert Einstein (1879–1955) German born American Physicist and Nobel Prize Winner

There were two separate conversations. At first glance, they appeared to have nothing to do with one another. The first girl was complaining how boys, and men for that matter, she added, could not make commitments. In her experience, guys were just reluctant to commit themselves to a relationship. None of the girls disagreed with her. None of the boys dared to argue.

The second conversation, an entirely unrelated conversation, unwittingly shed light on the first. A girl was explaining to her friend how she planned to have her education and her career, but then she planned to stay at home when the children came. There was nothing unusual about the choice she was making. All the girls and boys knew plenty of women who had made the same decision. It was a bit like choosing A, B, C, or D on a multiple choice test. There was nothing remarkable about it—for her. It is quite a different matter for him. And that, in part, explains why men can be so painstakingly slow in committing to a romantic relationship.

How is it different? Try imagining a man or a boy voicing the same desire, making the same choice as the girl who wished to ditch her career to stay home with the children. Rare is the man who thinks he has a choice. Even if he had the wherewithal to stay at home, it is difficult for men to make that choice and still think of themselves as **men**. There is no A, B, C, or D for him. It is taken for granted he will work. When the time comes, that is when he makes a commitment to the woman he loves, he will give up many of his dreams. It makes not one iota of difference that she may have a greater income than he does. He has made a commitment; his dreams are expected to take a backburner now. Putting his dreams on the back burner is part and parcel to making a commitment. She comes to the fore. And make no mistake about it, his dreams—his fantasies—are very different from hers.

Little girls, for instance, often fantasize about weddings. Girls imagine the dresses, the songs, and the flowers. They imagine it all right down to the last detail. They know what the groom will wear long before they know who the groom is. Often, they choose names for the children they hope to have. The groom is just the last piece of the puzzle.

Now I ask you—what boy fantasizes about weddings? None. Boys imagine there will be a wedding some day. Men do get married. It's been known to happen. They imagine there will be dresses, and songs, and flowers. They have heard the rumor. But this is hardly the stuff of fantasies. He lives in a different world. His fantasies are very different from hers. From Odysseus to James Bond to Indiana Jones, male fantasies are filled with adventure. Work is meaningful. The reasons for going to work reach far beyond the desire to bring home a paycheck. Things need doing. And **he** needs to do them. He has a sense of urgency. What he does is important. His country needs him. Picture James Bond alone beside the grave of his late wife. The woman has scarcely been interred when a helicopter arrives and a messenger with embarrassed apologies jumps out to tell our hero about a crisis back at the office. "They say it is **urgent**."

"It usually is," mutters James before being whisked away on another adventure of guns, girls and bad guys. Or think of brave Odysseus, the crafty hero of the Trojan War who must sleep with a beautiful goddess to save his men from her evil spell. It is a dirty job no doubt, but someone has to do it. His men must be saved. In his world, there are wrongs to be righted, enemies to be conquered, and always beautiful women to admire him. Life is good.

And then he decides to make a commitment, a big time commitment; he decides to marry. She comes first now. That's what commitment means. He has found the one he wants. And then everything changes. He has heard the rumor. He has it on good authority.

Ronald is a case in point. Ron was a teacher. His students and colleagues held him in high regard. He had a good rapport with his students. He connected with kids that other adults couldn't reach. He knew his job was something more than a way to make a living. It was rewarding work.

Ron met Helen through work. Helen was also a teacher. They dated and married. Ron continued for a while to work as a teacher just as he had planned. But all that Ron had been before he married Helen was no longer enough. Helen had ambitions for Ron. A teacher's salary wouldn't finance the lifestyle she envisioned. After all, his job was a reflection on her. And Ron had potential. Oh, he had so much potential. All he needed was a little push in the right direction. His red pen and papers would no longer be enough. What Ron needed was a job in the corporate world, something with a title. No more open collars. No more short sleeves. Ron needed a job where he wore a suit and tie and carried a brief case.

It wasn't long before Ron took a job in corporate America. He took a job as an executive assistant to the vice president. He went to work dressed like a Brooks Brothers model. He buckled on his sincerity suit. He cinched the knot of his power tie. He grabbed his briefcase and trotted off to work. Ron had a job that made Helen proud. His salary increased, and his sense of personal reward diminished. Helen beamed with pride at her successful husband. Ron felt miserable. This was not what he wanted. He felt like an ornament for Helen to wear.

Ron gave up the work he loved. He had responsibilities now. He had more to think about than himself. But his work wasn't the only thing he gave up. Slowly, the intimacy and devotion he had found so attractive with Helen before they married began to dissipate. And then the children came. The sex life he had enjoyed as a single man became infrequent and boring. He saw less and less of the woman who had made herself attractive for him and taken an interest in his day.

Ron feels like he gave up a lot for Helen. True, he has two lovely children, and he is devoted to them. But Ron misses the affection and respect he felt from Helen before they married. She no longer has much time for him, nor does she show much interest in what he does. He misses the rewarding work he used to do and the friends he used to keep company with. Ron loves Helen, but he is disappointed with the life he lives. Ron has settled for a life most men dread. "If it weren't for the children," he confided, "I'd leave."

Al and Tasha are another case in point. Al was a policeman. Ever since Al was a kid, he wanted to be a policeman. It was a job that meant something to him. It came with risks and he accepted them. The job could be very stressful too. And the hours, the hours were horrible. But as far as Al was concerned, it all came with the territory. Al was doing a job that needed doing. What he did mattered. And that made it all worthwhile.

Tasha admired Al in his smart uniform. She was proud of what he stood for. She listened to all his work stories. She even took an interest in his favorite sports teams. If Al was into it, Tasha was into it. Then, they married.

That's when the job became too dangerous for Tasha and the hours too terrible. That's when Tasha began to resent Al's time spent watching football. And one by one, she began to find fault in his friends and the time he spent with them.

Al is a claims adjuster for a popular insurance company now. Occasionally, he sees some of his former colleagues. He wonders how things might have been. "I think if I was still on the force, I might have made detective by now," he shrugs. "Who knows?"

Bob is reluctant to make a commitment. Bob is a successful lawyer. He has a fine home and drives a luxury car. The man has success written all over him. Bob is also fat and balding. "I always wonder if the women I go out with want to go out with me, or they want to go out with a lawyer. I want to be sure the woman I marry wants me for me."

Michael has this to add, "Please explain to women that men don't marry for sex. If he doesn't commit, it's because he hasn't found what he wants." That's true.

Comedian Jeff Foxworthy put it this way, "Getting married for sex is like buying a 747 for the free peanuts." Yeah, that is a bit expensive.

Still, men **do** commit to romantic relationships. Men get married every day. *Most men hope to make such a commitment*. And why would he not? After all, it means *he has found what he wants.*

"The Acid Test"

The Acid Test

A dame that knows the ropes isn't likely to get tied up.

—Mae West

I once heard a self-help guru suggest the quality of our lives is determined by the quality of the questions we ask ourselves. Good questions are important. I agree. I like good questions. But what I really like are good questions accompanied by good answers. Now that's helpful. And that leads us to your big question.

"Is this the right guy for me?" That's the question. And I can't answer it for you. I can, however, ask you some pretty good questions. You'll have to supply the answers.

Here is a clue. How does he act around his mother? Is he kind? Is he respectful? Is he considerate? If he doesn't behave well with his mother—and here we are talking about the woman who mothered him, who raised him, not necessarily his biological mother—he is not going to treat you well. Don't believe me? He treats you well, but not her? Wait for it. He will not treat you better than he treats his mother, not for long. Remember, the woman who raised him is his first love. How he behaves with her should tell you a lot. Pay attention.

What are his values? Would you like to be more like him? Think about it. We do rub off on each other. Over time, we become a bit like our partners.

Here is another idea. The next time you are at dinner some place he doesn't frequent, watch how he treats the wait staff. Is he a gentleman or is his behavior curt and difficult? When he deals with people he doesn't think he will see again, he will show his true colors. If he bullies and

---

brow beats them, watch out. If he bullies them, he will bully you. That is what bullies do.

Now here is the acid test. Would you like to have a son like this man? I didn't ask if you would like to have children; that's another question all together. I asked if you would be proud to have an adult son like this man. Think carefully. It is a big question. It is an important question. I didn't dream the question up. I heard it from an author named Barbara De Angelis, and I wish I had heard it long before I did, because if you change the question to read daughter instead of son, the question works just as well for men. This is a question that can help you avoid a lot of mistakes. If the quality of your life can be determined by the quality of the questions you ask yourself, this is one of the quality questions you need to ask. And it is a question you need to answer carefully and honestly.

Let me tell you a story. Several years ago, I knew a lady we will call Anna. Anna's situation was like that of many women. Anna was divorced. Her ex-husband had remarried, and she was raising their son. Her young son was a nice enough young fellow, but Anna was struggling. It was tough enough being a single mom, but there was more. Her little boy, who had spent very little time with his father, was very much like his father. He walked like his father. He gestured like his father. He even talked like his father. There wasn't anything wrong with any of these things, except that Anna couldn't stand the boy's father. And that was a problem, because while Anna felt obliged to love and care for her son, she didn't like him very much. She knew it was no fault of his. Still it was something she wrestled with. Anna's little boy was well on his way to becoming the kind of man she didn't like.

I'm not suggesting you want children or that you should want children. Still, it's worth thinking about. There were about 2.8 billion people in the world when I was a child. There are a bit more than six billion on the planet today. Babies happen. Sometimes, they happen quite unexpectedly. Children aren't an issue for you? Can't happen to you? Won't happen to you? The test is still valid.

If you would be proud to have a son like this man, you may have found your guy. If, on the other hand, this is not the kind of man you would want for a son, smile, say good bye, and keep walking. There are plenty of good guys out there. (About half of that six billion I was talking about are male.) Lots of women have good men in there lives, men they are proud of. And a lot of those women don't have as much to offer as you do. You deserve a man who is deserving of you. Don't settle for less.

www.ingramcontent.com/pod-product-compliance
Lightning Source LLC
Chambersburg PA
CBHW020355290526
45785CB00005B/2289